WHERE DO I LIVE?

STREET

A Crabtree Roots Book

ALICIA RODRIGUEZ

Crabtree Publishing
crabtreebooks.com

School-to-Home Support for Caregivers and Teachers

This book helps children grow by letting them practice reading. Here are a few guiding questions to help the reader with building his or her comprehension skills. Possible answers appear here in red.

Before Reading:

- What do I think this book is about?
    - *I think this book is about streets that people live on.*
    - *I think this book is about what you can see on your street.*
- What do I want to learn about this topic?
    - *I want to learn what kinds of buildings you can see on a street.*
    - *I want to learn how long a street can be.*

During Reading:

- I wonder why...
    - *I wonder why some streets have sidewalks, and some do not.*
    - *I wonder why cars are parked on some streets.*
- What have I learned so far?
    - *I have learned that houses can be found on streets.*
    - *I have learned that streets are found in neighborhoods.*

After Reading:

- What details did I learn about this topic?
    - *I have learned that many people use sidewalks.*
    - *I have learned that streets can be long or short.*
- Read the book again and look for the vocabulary words.
    - *I see the word* ***street*** *on page 3 and the word* ***neighborhood*** *on page 7. The other vocabulary words are found on page 14.*

My house is on
a **street**.

The street is very long

It is part of a **neighborhood**.

There are houses on it.

FLORIST & GIFT SHOP
Flowers
Gifts

There are **shops** on it.

There is a **sidewalk** that many people use

I like the street that
I live on.

Word List

Sight Words

a
are
house
I
is
it
like
long
many
my
of
on
part
that
there
use

Words to Know

neighborhood

shops

sidewalk

street

43 Words

My house is on a **street**.

The street is very long.

It is part of a **neighborhood**.

There are houses on it.

There are **shops** on it.

There is a **sidewalk** that many people use.

I like the street that I live on!

Written by: Alicia Rodriguez
Designed by: Rhea Wallace
Series Development: James Earley
Proofreader: Janine Deschenes
Educational Consultant: Marie Lemke M.Ed.

Photographs:
Shutterstock: Roschetzky Photography: cover; Jason Fin: p. 1; Shuttersv: p. 3, 14; Silvandia: p. 5; zstock: p. 6, 14; Ruchard Cavalieri; p. 9: Micheal Shake: p. 10, 14; Monkey Business Images: p. 12, 14

Crabtree Publishing

crabtreebooks.com 800-387-7650

 In Canada: We acknowledge the financial support of the Government of Canada through the Canada Book Fund for our publishing activities.

Printed in Canada/092023/CPC20230901

Published in Canada
Crabtree Publishing
616 Welland Avenue
St. Catharines, Ontario
L2M 5V6

Published in the United State
Crabtree Publishing
347 Fifth Avenue
Suite 1402-145
New York, NY 10016

Hardcover 978-1-4271-6002-7
Paperback 978-1-4271-6008-9
Ebook (pdf) 978-1-4271-3365-6
Epub 978-1-4271-3425-7
Read-along 978-1-4271-6026-3
Audio book 978-1-4271-6032-4

Library and Archives Canada Cataloguing in Publication

Title: Street / Alicia Rodriguez.
Names: Rodriguez, Alicia (Children's author), author.
Description: Series statement: Where do I live? |
"A Crabtree roots book".
Identifiers: Canadiana (print) 20210182857 |
Canadiana (ebook) 20210182865 |
ISBN 9781427160027 (hardcover) |
ISBN 9781427160089 (softcover) |
ISBN 9781427133656 (HTML) |
ISBN 9781427134257 (EPUB) |
ISBN 9781427160263 (read-along ebook)
Subjects: LCSH: Streets—Juvenile literature. |
LCSH: Neighborhoods—Juvenile literature.
Classification: LCC HT152 .R635 2022 | DDC j307.76—dc23

Library of Congress Cataloging-in-Publication Data

Names: Rodriguez, Alicia (Children's author) author.
Title: Street / Alicia Rodriguez.
Other titles: At head of title: Where do I live?
Description: New York, NY : Crabtree Publishing Company, [202
| Series: Where do I live? A Crabtree roots book |
Includes index.
Identifiers: LCCN 2021015129 (print) |
LCCN 2021015130 (ebook) |
ISBN 9781427160027 (hardcover) |
ISBN 9781427160089 (paperback) |
ISBN 9781427133656 (ebook) | ISBN 9781427134257 (epub) |
ISBN 9781427160263
Subjects: LCSH: Streets--Juvenile literature. | Neighborhoods--
Juvenile literature.
Classification: LCC HT152 .R6338 2022 (print) | LCC HT152
(ebook) | DD 307.76--dc23
LC record available at https://lccn.loc.gov/2021015129
LC ebook record available at https://lccn.loc.gov/2021015130